What Is
Science?

Dona Herweck Rice

Scientific Processes

observe

question

research

experiment

Measuring Equipment

scale

ruler

timer

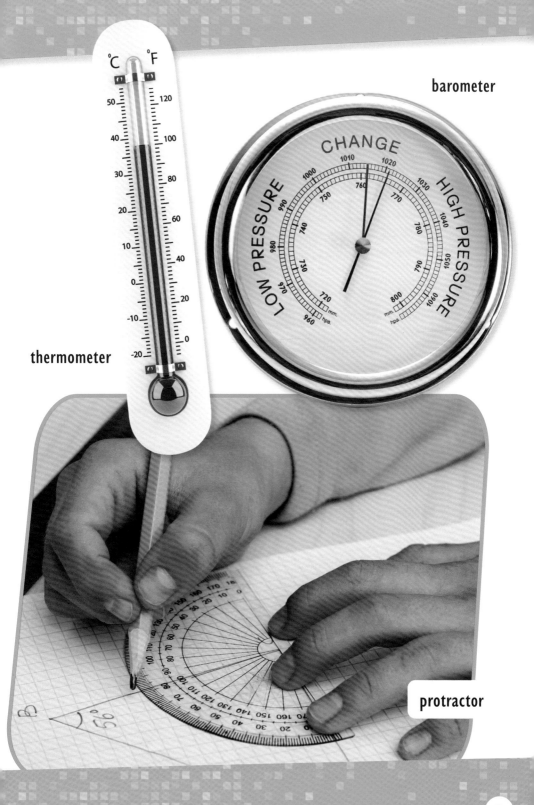

barometer

thermometer

protractor

Laboratory Equipment

goggles

glove

tongs

beaker

flask

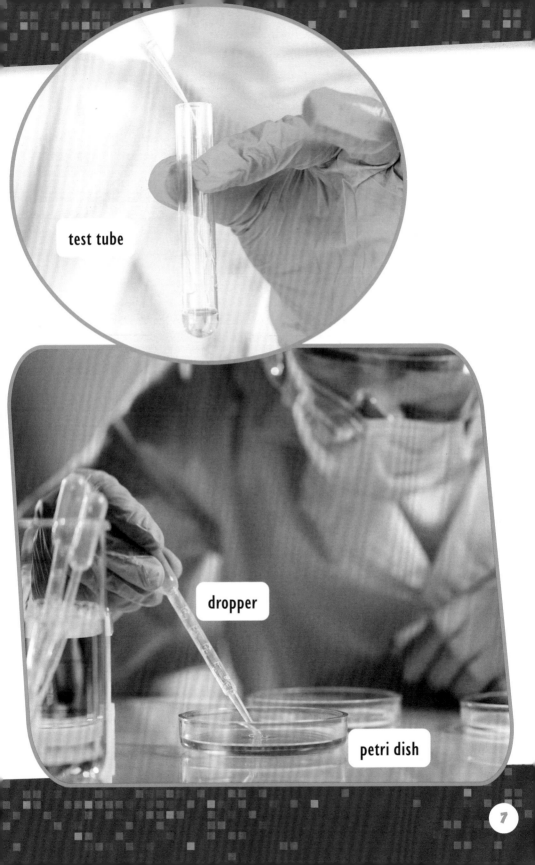

test tube

dropper

petri dish

Tools for Making Observations

microscope

slide

magnifying glass

recorder

camera

telescope

Equipment for Causing Change

valve

Bunsen burner

chemicals

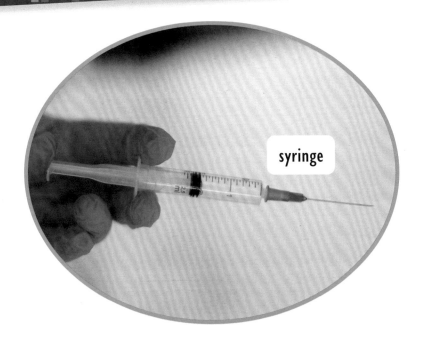

syringe

batteries

Simple Machines

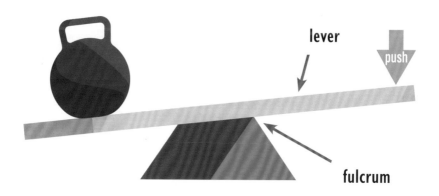

lever

push

fulcrum

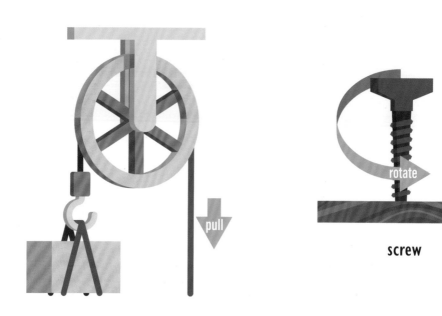

pull

rotate

screw

pulley

wedge

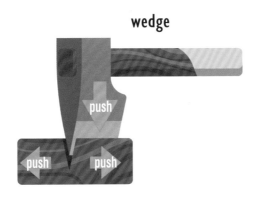

wheel

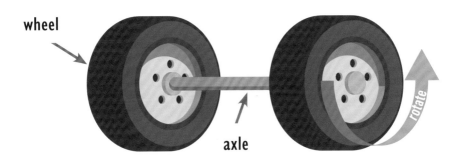

axle

inclined plane

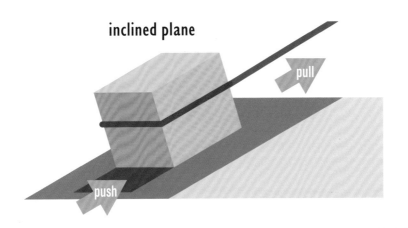

Solid

Liquid

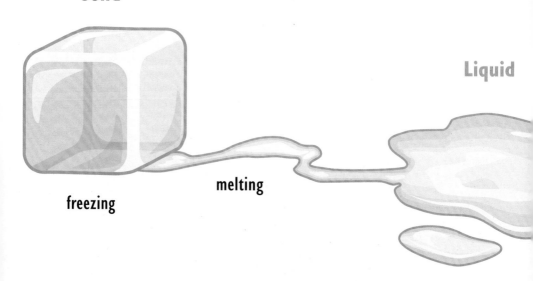

melting

freezing

Gas

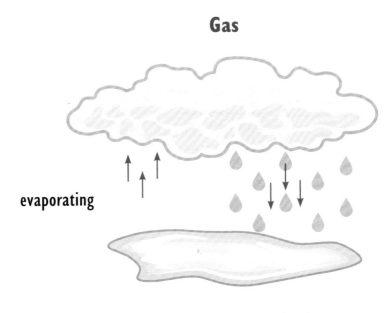

evaporating

condensing

Physical Science

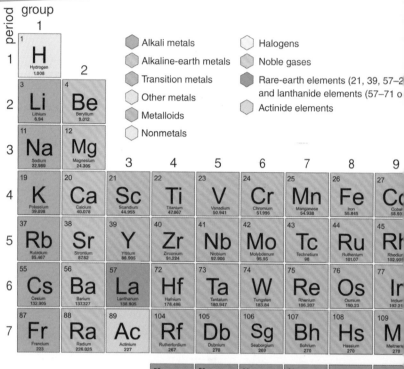

Legend	
Alkali metals	Halogens
Alkaline-earth metals	Noble gases
Transition metals	Rare-earth elements (21, 39, 57–2
Other metals	and lanthanide elements (57–71 o
Metalloids	Actinide elements
Nonmetals	

chemistry

Periodic Table

10	11	12	13	14	15	16	17	18
								2 He Helium 4.002
			5 B Boron 10.81	6 C Carbon 12.011	7 N Nitrogen 14.007	8 O Oxygen 15.999	9 F Fluorine 18.998	10 Ne Neon 20.179
			13 Al Aluminum 26.981	14 Si Silicon 28.085	15 P Phosphorus 30.973	16 S Sulfur 32.06	17 Cl Chlorine 32.06	18 Ar Argon 32.06
Ni Nickel 58.693	29 Cu Copper 63.546	30 Zn Zinc 65.38	31 Ga Gallium 69.723	32 Ge Germanium 72.630	33 As Arsenic 74.921	34 Se Selenium 78.971	35 Br Bromine 79.904	36 Kr Krypton 83.798
Pd Palladium 106.42	47 Ag Silver 107.868	48 Cd Cadmium 112.414	49 In Indium 114.818	50 Sn Tin 118.710	51 Sb Antimony 121.760	52 Te Tellurium 127.60	53 I Iodine 126.904	54 Xe Xenon 131.293
Pt Platinum 195.084	79 Au Gold 196.966	80 Hg Mercury 200.592	81 Tl Thallium 204.38	82 Pb Lead 207.2	83 Bi Bismuth 208.980	84 Po Polonium 209	85 At Astatine 210	86 Rn Radon 222
Ds armstadtium 281	111 Rg Roentgenium 281	112 Cn Copernicium 285	113 Nh Nihonium 286	114 Fl Flerovium 289	115 Mc Moscovium 289	116 Lv Livermorium 293	117 Ts Tennessine 293	118 Og Oganesson 294
Gd adolinium 157.25	65 Tb Terbium 158.925	66 Dy Dysprosium 162.500	67 Ho Holmium 164.930	68 Er Erbium 167.259	69 Tm Thulium 168.934	70 Yb Ytterbium 173.045	71 Lu Lutetium 174.966	
Cm Curium 247	97 Bk Berkelium 247	98 Cf Californium 251	99 Es Einsteinium 252	100 Fm Fermium 257	101 Md Mendelevium 258	102 No Nobelium 259	103 Lr Lawrencium 262	

atom

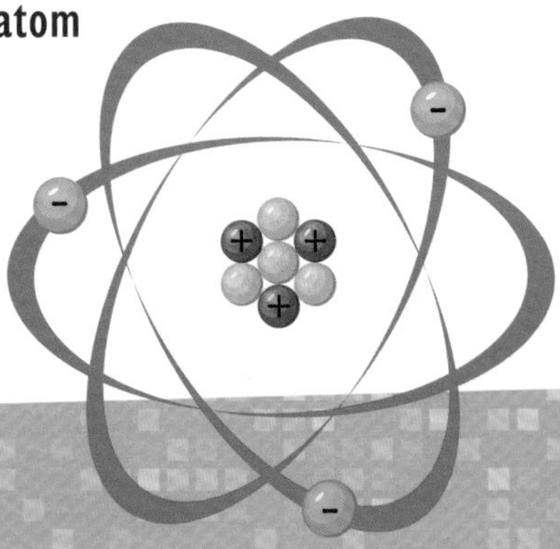

molecule

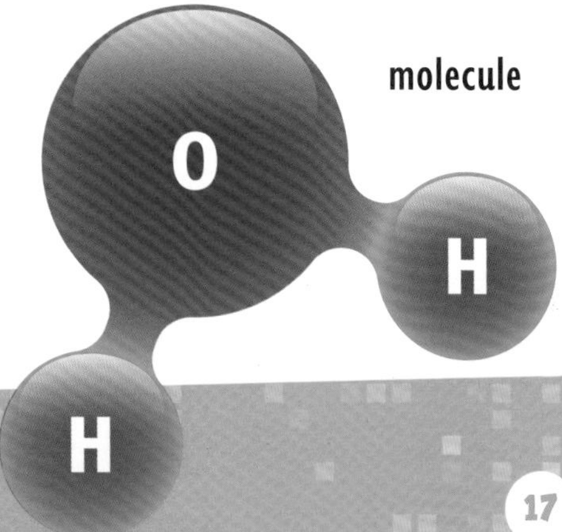

force → ← motion

gravity

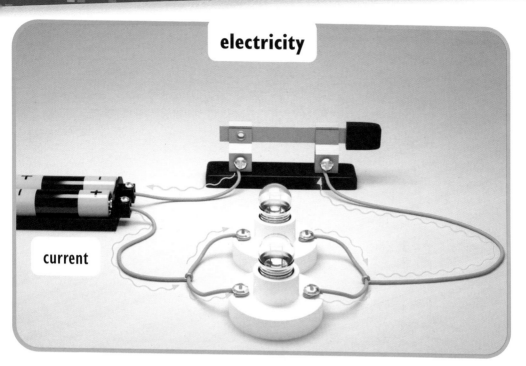

electricity

current

magnet

magnetism

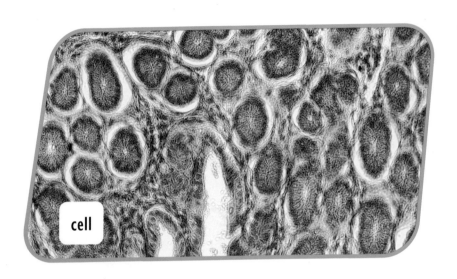

cell

plant cell diagram

animal cell diagram

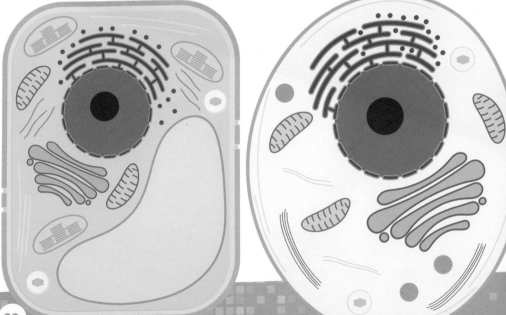

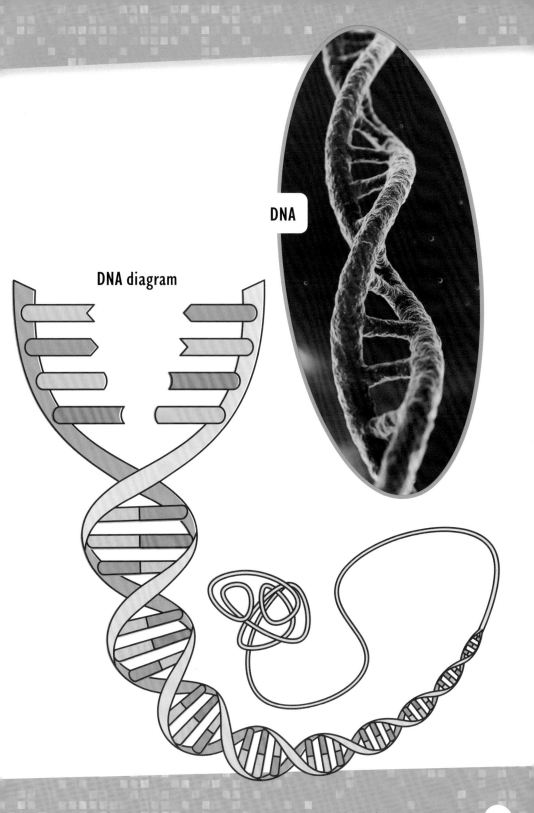

DNA

DNA diagram

Life Science

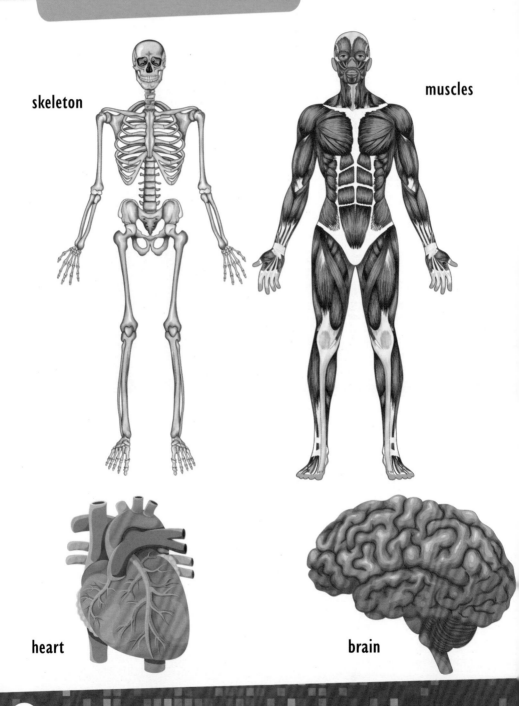

skeleton

muscles

heart

brain

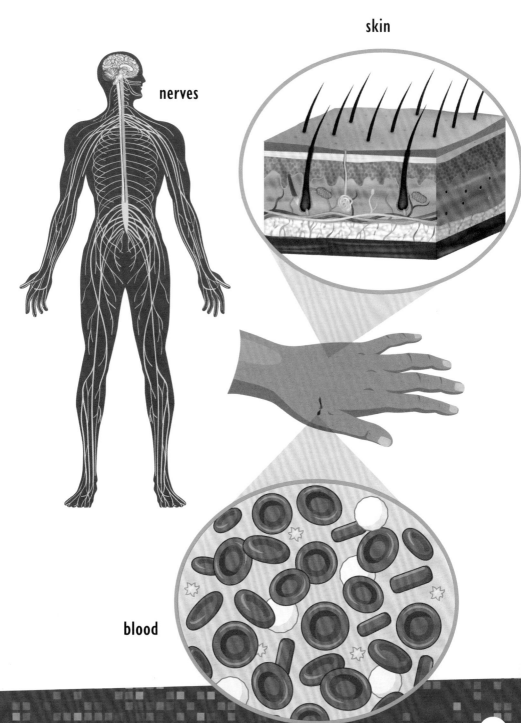

nerves

skin

blood

flowers

stem

leaves

roots

seeds

Photosynthesis

light energy

oxygen

carbon dioxide

sugar (glucose)

water

Earth

moon

planet

sun

star

comet

galaxy

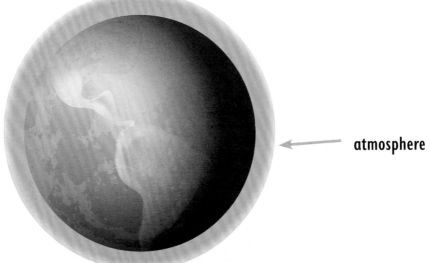

atmosphere

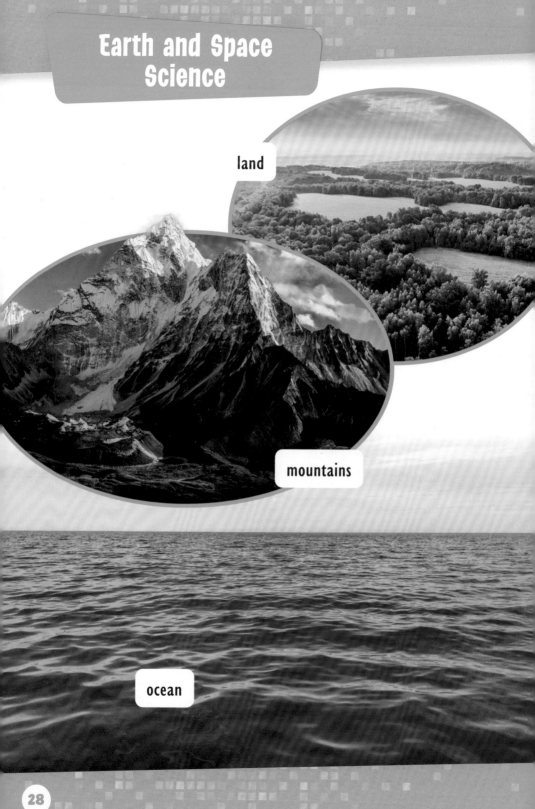

Earth and Space Science

land

mountains

ocean

valley

volcano

river

glacier

Earth and Space Science

desert

rain forest

tundra

grassland

forest

salt water

fresh water

Consultants

Cheryl Lane, M.Ed.
Secondary Teacher

Publishing Credits

Rachelle Cracchiolo, M.S.Ed., Publisher
Emily R. Smith, M.A.Ed., *SVP of Content Development*
Véronique Bos, *VP of Creative*
Jill Malcolm, *Senior Graphic Designer*

Image Credits: all images from iStock, Shutterstock, or in the public domain

Library of Congress Control Number available upon request.

5482 Argosy Avenue
Huntington Beach, CA 92649
www.tcmpub.com
ISBN 979-8-3309-0487-7
© 2025 Teacher Created Materials, Inc.
Printed by: 51497
Printed in: China

What Is Science?

Science is the study of the physical and natural world. Scientists observe the world around them and conduct experiments. They ask questions and discover answers to the mysteries of life and the universe.

ISBN-13: 979-8-3309-0487-7

90000

9 798330 904877

TCM Teacher Created Materials

156691